100 facts
Big Cats

100 facts Big Cats

Camilla de la Bedoyere

Consultant: Steve Parker

First published as hardback in 2005 by Miles Kelly Publishing Ltd
Bardfield Centre, Great Bardfield, Essex, CM7 4SL

Copyright © Miles Kelly Publishing Ltd 2005

4 6 8 10 9 7 5 3

This edition printed in 2009

Editorial Director: Belinda Gallagher
Art Director: Jo Brewer
Editor: Rosalind McGuire
Assistant Editor: Lucy Dowling
Volume Designers: Louisa Leitao/Alix Wood
Picture Researcher: Liberty Newton
Indexer: Jane Parker
Production Manager: Elizabeth Brunwin
Reprographics: Anthony Cambray, Stephan Davis,
Liberty Newton, Ian Paulyn
Editions Manager: Bethan Ellish

ISBN 978-1-84236-885-5

Printed in China

British Library Cataloguing-in-Publication Data
A catalogue record for this book is available from the British Library

ACKNOWLEDGEMENTS
Cover artwork by Martin Camm

The publishers would like to thank the following
sources for the use of their photographs:

Page 17(bl) Frans Lanting/Minden Pictures/FLPA; 27(tr) Gerard Lacz/FLPA;
40(b) Rob Reijnen/Foto Natura/FLPA; 41(tr) William Dow/Corbis;
45(tr) Frans Lanting/Minden Pictures/FLPA; 47(b) Martin B Withers/FLPA

All other images from the Miles Kelly Archives

Made with paper from a sustainable forest

www.mileskelly.net
info@mileskelly.net

www.factsforprojects.com
The one-stop homework helper — pictures, facts, videos, projects and more

Contents

Cats – cute or killers?

1 **All cats, big and small, are killers.** Their bodies are perfectly designed to find, chase and kill animals. Unlike other hunters, such as dogs and bears, cats only eat meat. They are the supreme predators of the animal world and are amongst the most intelligent, beautiful, graceful and athletic of all creatures on our planet. While small cats have found a place in our hearts and our homes, big cats are trying to survive in a world that is taking away the space and freedom they need.

Scientists divide the cat family into two groups.
Big cats can roar, but small cats can't.

▼ The agile caracal lives in Africa and the Middle East. It hunts rats, hares, birds and baby mammals such as antelope and wild pigs.

Big, bigger, biggest!

2 All members of the cat family are mammals. They are all strong but swift and most can climb trees easily. Their faces are rounded and their muzzles short. Cats are predators, which means that they hunt other animals and their teeth are suitable for catching, killing and eating their prey. All cats have excellent eyesight.

▲ The Siberian tiger is covered with thick fur that keeps it warm during the winter months.

3 The tiger is not only the biggest cat it is also one of the largest carnivores, or meat eaters, living on land. Of all tigers, Siberian tigers are the biggest. They may weigh as much as 350 kilograms and can measure 3 metres in length.

MAKE A MONSTER CAT

You will need:
2 cups plain flour 1 cup salt
1 cup water varnish or paint
bowl spoon
1. Put the flour into a bowl. Add the salt and water.
2. Mix to form a smooth dough and mould into a cat shape.
3. Put your models onto a greased baking tray. Bake at gas mark 1 or 120° C for one to three hours. Once cool, paint or varnish your model.

▲ A jaguar's spots look like rosettes and often have a dark smudge in the centre.

6 **The nimble cheetah does not need to be big to be successful.** It has developed into one of the world's greatest predators, proving that skill and speed can make up for a lack of bulky muscles.

7 **Sabre-toothed cats became extinct about 10,000 years ago.** *Smilodon* was the most famous sabre-toothed cat. It was the size of a large lion and its canine teeth were a massive 25 centimetres long!

4 **Jaguars are the biggest cats in the Americas.** They measure up to 2.7 metres in length and can weigh an impressive 158 kilograms, which makes them the third largest big cat.

5 **Lions hunt in groups called prides.** This means that they can catch much larger animals than other big cats that hunt alone. By living and hunting together all the lions in the group eat regularly. Male lions usually eat first, even though the females do most of the hunting.

▲ *Smilodon* probably stabbed thick-skinned animals with its huge teeth.

Where in the world?

8 **Big cats are found mainly in Africa, Eurasia and the Americas.** Where an animal lives is called its habitat. Big cats have adapted to live in a wide range of habitats, from sun-baked deserts to the snow-covered forests of Siberia. Most big cats live in hot countries where there are plenty of animals for them to hunt.

▼ There are about 37 species, or types, of cat found in the world today. Most cats are solitary forest-dwellers.

North America

South America

▶ North, Central and South America are known as the New World. Jaguars, ocelots, margays and pumas, such as the one shown here, are all found in this area.

9 **Jaguars and pumas are cats of the Americas, or New World.** While some jaguars are found in Central America, they have the best chance of surviving in the Amazon basin of Brazil. Here, the thick rainforest offers them protection from hunters. Pumas can live further north and south than any other species of large land mammal on Earth. They are found from the southernmost tip of Argentina, all the way north to Canada.

▲ The jaguar is best adapted to wetland habitats such as swamps and flooded forests.

◀ Tigers are only found in small regions of southern and eastern Asia. They live in a range of habitats, from tropical forests to Siberian woodlands.

Europe

Asia

Africa

▲ Cheetahs live in Africa and western Asia. Their habitat is open grasslands.

Oceania

▲ Lions live in Africa. A small number, called Asiatic lions, survive in the Gir Forest of southern Asia.

10 The mighty tiger once roamed from south and Southeast Asia, all the way to the Russian Far East. Now it only survives in little pockets of land in these areas. Tigers have lost their habitat to humans who want to farm and live on the land that was once ruled by these huge animals.

11 Millions of years ago the Americas were joined to Europe, Africa and Asia. The ancestors of modern cats were able to move across this huge landmass. But Australia, New Zealand and New Guinea separated from the other continents before cats appeared. That is why no cats are native to these places.

12 Africa is home to many big cats including cheetahs, lions and leopards. Lions live on vast grasslands called the savannah. Their pale fur is the perfect colour to blend in with the dried grasses of the open plains. Cheetahs also hunt on the savannah, but tend to do so during the day, when the other big cats are resting.

King of the jungle

▶ Lions are often incorrectly referred to as 'Kings of the jungle'. However, it is tigers, not lions, that are at home in this environment. Tigers are endangered, which means that if we do not do enough to save them, they may soon become extinct.

13 **The tiger is the largest of all the cats and also one of the hardest to find.** Tigers live deep in the jungle where huge trees block out the sunlight, helping them to blend into the murky darkness. Their stripes camouflage them as they tread silently through the dappled shadows. This coat is also perfect for hiding the tiger in long grass.

14 **Tigers hunt by stealth.** They hunt at night, when they can creep up on their prey. Tigers may travel several kilometres each night, roaming along tracks, searching for their victims. Tigers hunt for deer, wild pigs, cattle, monkeys and reptiles. They will even kill young elephants or rhinoceroses.

15 **Tigers love swimming.** When it is hot they may take a dip in lakes and rivers to cool down. They are good swimmers and can make their way across large stretches of water.

16

Although they are powerful hunters, tigers may have to stalk 20 animals before they manage to catch just one. They normally kill once every five to six days and eat up to 40 kilograms of meat in one go! Tigers often return to a kill for several days until they have finished it, or scavengers have carried it away.

▼ People who need to go into the tigers' forest in Sundarban in east India and Bangladesh, wear masks on the back of their heads. This confuses the tigers into leaving them alone.

QUIZ

1. Why do tigers have stripes?
2. What name is given to animals that eat food that's been left by others?
3. If you were walking in a tiger's forest, how could you try to keep yourself safe?

Answers:
1. A stripy coat helps to camouflage them in the forest. 2. Scavengers, e.g. hyenas and vultures. 3. You could wear a mask on the back of your head

18

No two tigers have the same pattern on their coats. White tigers with black stripes are occasionally seen in the wild and are bred in zoos because they are very popular with visitors. Although they don't look like their parents, these tigers are not different in any other way.

▶ White tigers are rare in the wild. This white tiger cub is less likely to survive because its coat does not provide good camouflage.

17

Bengal tigers have a reputation as 'man-eaters'. Tigers don't usually eat people unless they are too sick or old to find other prey, but some tigers prefer the taste of human flesh. Between 1956 and 1983, more than 1500 people were killed by tigers in one region alone.

Jaws and claws

19 **Animals have teeth that are best suited to the types of food they eat.** Cats have long, sharp front teeth to bite and kill their prey. They also have strong back teeth to tear and chew pieces of meat.

20 **Catching, killing and eating other animals is a tough job.** In order to be successful hunters, cats need to have special teeth. Their pointy teeth are called canines. These are especially good for killing or holding onto prey. Behind the canines are carnassials. These teeth are ultra-sharp and they work like a pair of scissors to slice up flesh.

▼ This leopard has killed a gazelle. Leopards drag their prey up into trees where it is out of the reach of other hungry predators and scavengers.

21 Cat tongues are very rough! The scratchy surface is ideal for scraping meat off bones. Cats can make their tongues into a scoop shape, which means that they can take big gulps of water when they are thirsty.

▶ Each claw on this lion's paw is curved and very sharp – a perfect tool for digging into its prey.

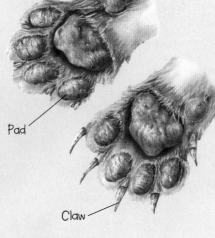

Pad

Claw

◀ A cat's tongue feels rough because it is covered in hard spikes, or papillae.

22 The paws of big cats and pet cats are very similar. All cats have paws that are armed with sharp, deadly daggers – claws. The bottom surface of each paw has soft pads that are surrounded by tufty fur to muffle the sound of every footstep.

True or false?

1. Cats can make their tongues into a scoop shape.
2. Cats have five claws on their back paws.
3. The spikes on a cat's tongue are called papillae.

Answers:
1. True 2. False – they have four 3. True

Going solo

23 Most cats are loners. Each animal has its own patch of ground, or territory, which it lives in and defends. Youngsters normally stay with their mother until they are between one and three years old. Then they have to look out for themselves. Lions, however, normally live in groups called prides.

◀ A fight between two leopards over a territory can be extremely fierce and can even be a fight to the death.

24 Lions live together. No one knows why lions live in groups. It may have something to do with their habitat. Hunting on the open grasslands might be easier in a group. Also, it's hard to hide your supper from scavengers, such as hyenas and vultures, when there are few bushes and trees. Maybe a group of lions can send a pack of nosy hyenas on their way more easily than a lion could on its own.

I DON'T BELIEVE IT!

Young male lions get thrown out of the pride at about three years old, and spend their 'teenage' years roaming the plains, alone or with their brothers and cousins.

25 Cats mark their territory with their scent, which tells other cats to stay away. They do this by spraying urine on trees and bushes around their area. If another cat comes into their territory there may be a fight. Usually, big cats roar at intruders to scare them away rather than fight.

► By washing its face, this cheetah cub is putting scent from glands in its chin onto its paws. It can then mark its territory as it walks.

26 Cats' fur also carries a strong scent. Their scent is made by special parts of their body called glands. When cats wash they spread this smell all over their bodies, and as they rub against trees, the smell comes off. This is another way of marking their territory. That is why pet cats rub themselves against your legs – they are making it clear to other cats that you belong to them!

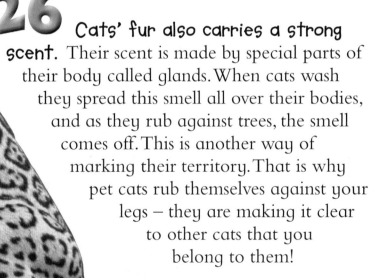

◄ Cats patrol their territories regularly. This jaguar is sniffing a tree to check that its scent is still strong.

Spotted sprinter

27 Cheetahs are the world's fastest land animals and can run as fast as a car. Within 2 seconds of starting a chase, a cheetah can reach speeds of 75 kilometres an hour, and it soon reaches a top speed of about 105 kilometres an hour. Cheetahs run out of energy after only 30 seconds of sprinting, so if its prey can keep out of the cheetah's jaws for this amount of time, it may escape capture.

28 This big cat lives in the grasslands and deserts of Africa and Middle East and Western Asia. Cheetahs do not often climb trees, as they have difficulty in getting down again. Cubs often hide in bushes so that they can surprise their prey. The word 'cheetah' means 'spotted wind' – the perfect name for this speedy sprinter.

▼ Cheetahs prefer wide open spaces where they can easily spot prey such as gazelles.

29 Like most of the big cats, cheetahs often live alone. Females live in an area called their 'home range', only leaving if food is scarce. When cubs leave their mothers they often stay together in small groups. Eventually the females go off to find their own home ranges, but the cubs may stay together and attack other cheetahs that come too close.

▶ Cheetah mothers keep their cubs hidden until they are old enough to start learning how to hunt.

30 There are usually between four and six cubs in one litter. Sadly, only one cub in every 20 lives to be an adult cheetah. The others are usually killed by lions or hyenas.

31 Cubs have thick tufts of long, white fur on their heads, necks and shoulders. No one knows why they have this hair, but it might make them look bigger and stronger than they really are.

32 Cheetahs kill antelopes by biting their throats, stopping them from getting any air. Cheetahs can spend a whole day eating if they are undisturbed by vultures or lions, which will steal the food if they can.

How fast are these animals?
Put them in order of fastest to slowest:
1. Cheetah 2. Kangaroo
3. Spur-winged goose
4. Thompson's gazelle

Answers: 1 3 4 2

Home on the range

33 Thousands of years ago, nearly half the world's land was covered in grasslands. Since then much of it has been built upon or turned into farmland. This has contributed to the falling numbers of big cats in these areas. Some grasslands are now protected. These places have become sanctuaries for wildlife.

34 Grasslands occur in places where it's too hot for trees, but there is enough rain to stop the land turning into desert. This is called the savannah and it is home to some of the most famous big cats. When it rains, the waterholes fill and the grass grows green. During the dry seasons, the Sun scorches the grass to the colour of sand and big cats struggle to find enough water and food to survive.

35 **Grass is the favourite food of animals that graze.** Animals such as giraffes, antelope and wildebeest nibble at the grass, or pick leaves off the bushes and trees that litter the plain.

I DON'T BELIEVE IT!
There are now only 12,000 cheetahs left in Africa, and no more than 200 in Western Asia. Many have been killed for their beautiful fur.

◄ Life in open grassland is difficult and dangerous for plant-eaters. There are few places to hide from hunters such as cheetahs and lions.

36 **Zebra and other grazing animals make a tasty meal for lions and cheetahs.** Since there are few trees to hide behind, it is difficult for these big cats to surprise their prey. Cheetahs rely on speed to catch other animals, while lions hunt in a group. These big cats watch a herd of zebra for some time before making their move. They try to spot any creature that is particularly small, weak or old. If they can separate this animal from the rest of the herd, it will be easier to kill.

Cub class

37 **Cubs are born helpless and blind.** A group of cubs is called a litter and there are usually between two and four in each one. Cubs depend on their mother's milk for the first few months of life, but gradually their mother will introduce them to titbits of meat that she brings back to the den.

▲ Lion cubs, may stay with their mothers for two years or more before beginning an independent life.

▶ Mother cats such as this puma need to stay alert and on the lookout for danger. Their cubs, or kittens, make an easy target for other predators.

38

Male lions help to look after their young. When the lionesses are hunting, the males protect the cubs and play with them. When a hunt is successful the males eat before the females, but often let the cubs eat first. All lions have black tufts of fur on the ends of their tails. The tufts don't seem to have any use except as playthings for lion cubs!

▼ Lion cubs like to play. Even this tortoise is a source of interest. By playing like this, the cubs are learning hunting skills.

39

The babies of some cats, such as pumas, are called kittens. Adult pumas are sand-coloured, to provide them with camouflage in the deserts and mountains where they live. Their kittens are born with spots on their fur that gradually fade. Spots are better camouflage for these youngsters, which hide in bushes and undergrowth.

40

Cubs learn how to hunt from watching their mothers. Many mother cats teach their babies how to hunt by bringing them small animals that they have captured alive. When they let the animal loose, the cubs or kittens can play with it and practise their hunting skills. It may seem cruel, but it is important that the cubs learn how to look after themselves.

I DON'T BELIEVE IT!

Cubs have a tough time making it to adulthood. Cubs are hidden by their mothers, partly to avoid bumping into any males. Male cats such as tigers kill any cubs that aren't their own.

Sociable simba

41 **Lions are sociable animals.** They live in family groups called prides that normally include between four and six adults, all related, and their cubs. Large prides of perhaps 30 animals develop where there is plenty of food.

▶ Lionesses give birth to a litter of between one and six cubs. The cubs stay with their mother for over two years.

42 **Unlike other big cats, male and female lions look very different.** They both have sandy-coloured fur that blends into sun-scorched grasslands, but the males have manes of darker hair on their heads and shoulders that make them look powerful and threatening.

43 **The best time to hunt is early morning or evening.** The lionesses prepare an ambush by spreading out and circling their prey. They hunt zebra, wildebeest, impala and buffalo. A group of lionesses has been known to bring down an adult giraffe that was 6 metres tall!

44 Although it is unusual, lions do sometimes attack and eat humans. In the 1930s and 1940s, a family of lions in Tanzania preferred human flesh to the normal lion diet of antelope. They killed nearly 1500 people in just 15 years.

I DON'T BELIEVE IT!
Every cat's favourite pastime is napping. Lions spend almost 80 percent of their time sleeping, lying down or sitting doing nothing!

45 Adult males only stay with their pride for a few years at a time. If a male wants to become the leader of another pride, it must fight the males and kill the cubs. This seems very cruel, but it does this to make the lionesses ready to have more cubs before it mates with them. The new leader then knows that all the cubs in the pride will be their own.

46 Few animals would dare to attack a healthy lion. When a lion has become old and weak, however, it may be easy prey for a band of hyenas. It is said that lions only fear hyenas – this is because they know they could end up in the bellies of several of them!

Jungle cats

47 More than half of the world's wild cats live in forests and jungles. In some of these forests, the weather remains hot and wet all year round. In others there are long dry spells, followed by periods of heavy rain. These rainy seasons are known as monsoons. Both types of forest are packed full of animal and plant life.

◄ Jaguars live in South American rainforests, but often stray onto farmland and prey on domestic cattle.

▼ Tigers prefer wet habitats and they are strong swimmers.

48 Tigers hide in tall grass and thick vegetation. As the sunlight and shadows flicker on the tiger's stripy fur, it blends into the background. It moves little during the day and spends most of its time resting. As the sun fades, it creeps through the forest, its paws softly padding across the forest floor. It is looking and listening for any animal that it may catch unawares.

50 Some jungle areas are protected and people are not allowed to cut down the trees. These areas are called 'reserves' and are meant to provide a place where animals, including all kinds of big cats, can live safely in peace.

49 Leopards are skilful hunters. Despite this, they are becoming increasingly rare in rainforest areas due to the destruction of their habitat.

Quiz

Look at this list of jungle animals and decide whether each is a bird, mammal or reptile:
1. Toucan 2. Python
3. Gibbon 4. Vulture
5. Margay 6. Turtle

Answers:
Birds: toucan and vulture
Mammals: gibbon and margay
Reptiles: turtle and python

Swift and sure

51 Big cats move in a similar way to smaller cats. They are very athletic and are able to run, climb, pounce and leap almost silently. These skills are important because when hunting they need to get as close to their prey as they can before attacking it.

▼ All cats run in a similar way. They push off with both hind legs together but land on one front foot and then the other.

Domestic cat

Cheetah

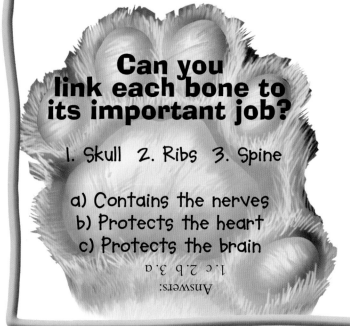
Can you link each bone to its important job?

1. Skull 2. Ribs 3. Spine

a) Contains the nerves
b) Protects the heart
c) Protects the brain

Answers:
1.c 2.b 3.a

52 Cheetahs are the fastest of all cats. Their spines, or backbones, are so bendy they can bring their hind legs forward between their front paws when they run. This means that they can take huge steps as they bound forwards. Unlike most cats, they do not have retractable claws on their feet. When they run their claws stick into the ground like the spikes on an athlete's shoes.

53 Some cats, such as leopards, spend a lot of their time in trees. Long tails help them to keep their balance as they move along narrow branches. They can chase monkeys high up into a tree, keeping their footing on branches that seem too flimsy to support a squirrel! If the monkey falls the leopard will turn and race headfirst down the tree to reach its prey.

▶ When tree-climbing cats like caracals fall from a height they can usually regain their balance and land on their feet.

1. The caracal may lose its footing as it chases prey along branches

2. It has a superb sense of balance and quickly begins to right itself

3. A flexible spine helps the falling caracal twist its body

4. Cats' muscles are very strong and their joints are very flexible so the caracal can absorb the shock of hitting the ground to give it a 'soft landing'

54 Do cats really have nine lives? It often seems that cats can survive almost any scrape they get themselves into. They don't have nine lives but their strength and quick reactions can save their lives. When a cat falls out of a tree, it can twist its body round so that it lands on its feet – and walk away with its head held high and a flick of its tail!

American athlete

▲ Pumas live in the New World, from the southern tip of South America all the way to Alaska.

I DON'T BELIEVE IT!
Though large in size, the puma is not one of the seven species of 'big cats', so it cannot roar. Instead, it makes an ear-piercing scream which scares both humans and animals alike!

screeech!

55 **The puma is a great athlete.** Pumas have long hind legs packed with muscles – ideal for jumping, running and climbing. Of all the big cats, these are the most graceful. They can spring 2 metres into a tree then bound up a further 18 metres before leaping down to the ground.

56 Pumas are known by a variety of names including cougar, panther, red jaguar, mountain screamer, catamount, deer tiger and mountain lion. People from Central and South America call them *chimblea*, *miztil*, *pagi* or *leopardo*.

57 When you live in a hot climate and are covered in a coat of fur, it can be difficult to keep cool. Pumas, like other cats, pant to lose heat. When an animal pants, it opens its mouth and lets its tongue hang out. This means that water can evaporate off the surface of the tongue, lowering the animal's body temperature.

58 Rabbits, mice, rats and hares are popular prey for pumas. They will also attack larger mammals, including deer, cattle and elks. In some places, humans have built houses in or near the pumas' natural habitat. This has resulted in people being attacked – even killed – by these wild animals. Now, people are beginning to realize that they have to respect the pumas' natural instincts and stay away from their territory.

59 These big cats are highly skilled killers. They hunt by slowly creeping up on an unsuspecting victim. When ready, they pounce, knocking their prey to the ground in one sudden hit. A single, swift bite kills the puma's victim immediately.

▼ Pumas often hunt small animals, such as hares, squirrels, beavers and turkeys.

60 Although pumas can kill porcupines, it is not an easy task. They need to flip the prickly creature onto its back before biting its soft belly. If the porcupine manages to spear the puma with one of its many spines, the wound may prove fatal.

◄ The North American porcupine can climb trees and has a crest of long spines, or quills, on its head and back.

Life in a cold climate

61 **There are no wild cats living in the Antarctic.** Maybe the weather is too cold for them or there are too few animals to eat. Some big cats do live in cold climates. Like all animals that live in these remote areas, they grow thick fur and store extra layers of fat under their skin to keep warm.

62 **The beautiful snow leopard lives in one of the most challenging habitats in the world.** It roams a mountainous area of Central Asia where the weather is cold and few plants are able to grow. Snow leopards live alone and travel across a huge area searching for food.

I DON'T BELIEVE IT!

While Siberian tigers survive winters at temperatures as low as −33°C, the Bengal tigers try to keep cool in hot forests where temperatures can reach a sweltering 38°C!

63 Snow leopards hunt yaks, asses, sheep and goats as well as smaller mammals and birds. They survive the extreme cold because they have very thick fur, especially in winter. They also wrap their long tails around their bodies when they sleep to keep in heat. A snow leopard's grey coat helps to camouflage it in snow. During the summer, snow leopards often take a dip in mountain streams to cool themselves down.

64 Siberian tigers live in cold climates in Russia and China. Their coats are pale with brown stripes, rather than the more common black stripes. During the winter months their fur grows long, thick and shaggy to help keep them warm. They hunt other creatures that live in this harsh climate, such as wild boar, moose, sika deer and bears.

▼ Despite its name the snow leopard is quite different from other leopards. It is smaller and its coat is much paler and thicker.

Super senses

▼ Cats have eyes on the front of their heads. Eyes in this position are best placed for judging distance. This jaguar has fantastic night vision but its colour vision is not as good as ours.

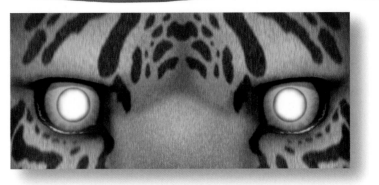

▲ Cats' eyes appear to glow in the dark because they have a layer of cells that reflect light.

65 At night, cats can see four times better than humans. This is because they have a layer at the back of the eye that reflects light. This helps cats to see things clearly in low light.

66 All cats have flexible ears that they can turn towards any sounds they hear. Cats also use their ears to show how they are feeling. An angry cat will lower and twist its ears so that they are lying almost flat against its head.

67 Cats sniff their food before eating to check it is not bad or poisonous. They also sniff the bushes and trees in their territories to discover if any other animals have passed by.

The pupils in a cat's eye close up when the cat is angry and open up wide when it is frightened.

▶ Clouded leopards use their whiskers to help them find their way through dense jungle vegetation, especially at night.

68 A cat's whiskers are special hairs that are extra-sensitive. They are particularly useful at night when it is likely to be hunting. As the cat moves through undergrowth, its whiskers brush against the leaves, helping it choose a safe path. It is only by using all of their senses together that cats are able to move about easily in darkness.

▼ Despite their doglike appearance hyenas are more closely related to cats than dogs.

69 Cats use all of their senses to stay alive. As hunters, they need to be able to find, chase and catch their prey. Although big cats do not have many natural enemies, they need to watch out for scavengers, such as hyenas. These animals gang up on big cats and steal their meals.

A coat to die for

70 The jaguar is the owner of a beautiful fur coat – so beautiful that many people want to own it too. Although it is against the law to capture a jaguar for its skin, they are still hunted. Jaguars live in rainforests, often in areas where farmers are cutting back trees to grow crops. As jaguars' habitats continue to shrink, so will their numbers.

71 At first glance a jaguar looks like a leopard, but it is possible to tell them apart by a few tell-tale differences. A jaguar's head is bigger and rounder than a leopard's, with round ears not pointed ones. Its tail is quite a bit shorter than the leopards and its shoulders are broad and packed with muscle.

72 Of all the big cats jaguars are the most water-loving. They like swampy areas, or places that flood during wet seasons. Jaguars are strong swimmers and seem to enjoy bathing in rivers. They live in Central and South America but less than a hundred years ago, they were living as far north as California and Texas.

▼ Jaguars are similar to leopards but they have broader shoulders, shorter legs and larger heads. All jaguars love water.

73 Young jaguars climb trees where they hunt for birds and small mammals. As they grow bigger they become too heavy for the branches. Adults tend to stay on the ground, or in water, to hunt.

▲ A capybara's eyes, ears and nose are on the top of its head so that it can spot a lurking predator as it wallows in water.

74 Jaguars hunt a wide range of animals including deer, tapirs, birds, fish and capybaras. Capybaras are the world's heaviest rodent and can measure up to 130 centimetres in length.

◄ Jaguars can feed on turtles because they have large, heavy teeth and immensely powerful jaws.

I DON'T BELIEVE IT!

In one year alone, at least 13,500 jaguars were killed for their coats. Today, the future of the jaguar is most at risk from the destruction of its rainforest habitat.

75 Jaguars' powerful jaws are so strong that they can crack open the hard shells of turtles and tortoises. These cats will even kill large animals, such as cattle and horses. It is their habit of killing cows that upsets many people who share the jaguars' territory. Cattle are very important to the farmers, who may poison or shoot jaguars that are killing their livestock.

Spots and stripes

Tiger fur

Cheetah fur

▲ The top layer of a cat's coat is made of coarse, long hair. It is this hair that is coloured and carries the pattern.

76 Patterned fur has helped cats survive, but it may be the death of them. For centuries, people have hunted cats for their beautiful coats. In some cases this has brought big cats to the edge of extinction.

77 A cat's fur keeps it warm when the weather is cold and cool when it is too hot. The fur is made up of two layers – a short and fluffy bottom layer and a top layer that is made of longer coloured fur.

▼ No one really knows why a lion's coat is generally plain tawny, while cheetahs and leopards, which live in similar habitats in Africa, are spotted. This lion's coat enables it to almost disappear into the long grass.

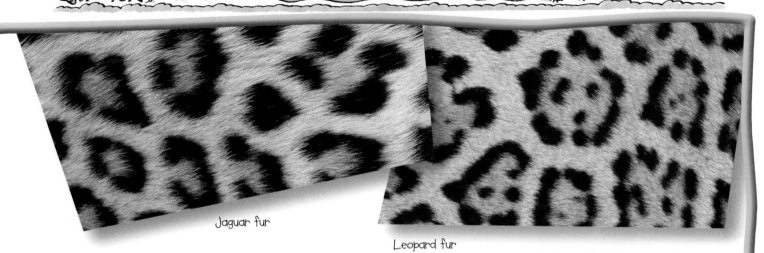

Jaguar fur

Leopard fur

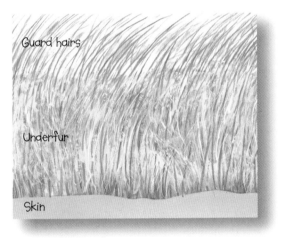

Guard hairs

Underfur

Skin

◀ The layer of soft, downy fur next to a cat's skin traps air and helps to keep the cat warm.

QUIZ
1. What is the only big cat that has stripes when it is an adult?
2. Name a grass-eating animal that has stripes.
3. Which big cat has rosettes with dark centres?

Answers:
1. Tiger 2. Zebra 3. Jaguar

78 The pattern on a cat's coat helps it to blend in with its surroundings. This is called camouflage. Spots blend in with the effect of dappled sunlight, stripes with long grasses.

▼ White patches are clearly visible on the backs of this tiger's ears.

79 Many big cats have white patches on their ears. This may help cubs to follow their mother in dark forest. Cats that are angry or scared usually flatten their ears and twist them so that the patches can be seen from the front. This may warn other cats to stay away.

Supercat

▲ There are probably more leopards in the wild than all the other big cats put together. This success has earned leopards the nickname 'supercat'.

80 Leopards can live close to humans but never be seen by them. They live in Africa and as far east as Malaysia, China and Korea. Leopards hunt by night and sleep in the day. They are possibly the most common of all the big cats, but are rarely seen in the wild.

81 Leopards may sit in the branches of a tree, waiting patiently for their meal to come to them. As their prey strolls past, the leopard drops from the branches and silently, quickly, kills its victim.

82 Leopards nearly always hunt at night. A leopard approaches its prey in absolute silence, making sure that it does not snap a twig or rustle leaves. With incredible control, it places its hind paws onto the exact places where its forepaws had safely rested. When it is within striking distance of its victim it will attack.

83

Leopards are not fussy eaters. They will eat dung beetles, frogs or birds if nothing better comes along. They prefer to hunt monkeys, pigs and antelopes.

◄ Dung beetles feed on dung and lay their eggs in it. They make a crunchy snack for hungry leopards.

84

Once a leopard has caught its meal, it does not want to lose it to passing scavengers such as hyenas or jackals. The leopard might climb up a tree, hauling its prey with it. It may choose to eat immediately or store the animal for later. Hiding food like this is called 'caching' (known as 'cashing').

85

Although the name 'panther' is usually given to pumas, it is also used for leopards that have black fur. Black panthers are not a different type of leopard – some cubs are simply born with black fur rather than the normal tawny-brown hide.

◄ If you could get close enough to a black panther you would see that its fur is spotted.

41

Scaredy cat

86 **The world's most mysterious cat is the clouded leopard.** It is very shy and very rare. In fact, it is difficult to say how many of these pretty creatures are alive today, it is so unusual to even spot one! It is about 2 metres in length, half of which is its tail, which it uses to help balance in the trees.

87 **Clouded leopards are excellent climbers and live in the forests of Southeast Asia, from Nepal to southern China.** As it was once believed that they spent most of their time in trees, they were given the name 'tree cats' in Malaysia. Scientists studying them now think that they also live in grassland and mangrove swamps, and spend at least as much time on the ground as they do in the trees. Clouded leopards eat wild boar, monkeys and deer, which they catch by stalking.

88 The clouded leopard is a big cat that behaves like a little cat! It can jump around in trees as easily as a domestic tabby. These agile animals have been seen running headfirst down a tree trunk and even hanging upside-down by their hind feet. If that isn't enough, these gymnasts like swimming too!

I DON'T BELIEVE IT!

Clouded leopards can leap distances of more than 5 metres as they clamber through the treetops of their forest home.

◄ Little is known about clouded leopards. They sleep all day and only hunt at night. Despite their length, these cats weigh only about 20 kilograms – roughly the same as a six-year-old child.

89 While no one knows how many clouded leopards there are left in the wild, experts agree that their numbers are declining. This is partly because their habitat is being destroyed, but they are also being hunted for their fur. Their teeth and bones are used in traditional Asian medicines. Sadly, clouded leopards do not live happily in zoos either, rarely breeding in captivity.

Cat cousins

▼ The African serval often hunts water voles in the reeds and rushes that surround lakes and waterholes.

90 Several types of small wild cat live around the world. There are about 37 types, or species, of cat – big and small. Added to this there are 300 breeds of domestic (pet) cat. Whether they are big or small, all cats are natural-born predators.

91 One of the world's bounciest cats is the serval. It can leap one metre high and travel a distance of 4 metres as it jumps like a jack-in-the-box to strike at its prey. All this effort may be for a small supper of frogs or locusts, which are some of the serval's favourite titbits.

92 The serval is unusual because it hunts during the day. Most cats prefer to hunt at night or during the dimly-lit hours of morning or evening. Servals live in the African savannah and look very similar to cheetahs, with a slim, graceful body and long, slender forelimbs.

93 **Like its neighbour the jaguar the ocelot has been hunted for its fur.** It lives in the forests, grasslands and swamps of South America. Ocelots usually live alone or in pairs and will eat almost anything they can catch. Until the hunting of these extraordinary cats was made illegal, as many as 200,000 pelts (skins) were sold every year.

▶ The ocelot is extremely agile and can leap from the ground on a dark night and grab a low–flying bat in its paws or mouth.

94 **The lynx can change its coat according to the weather.** In fact its winter coat looks so different from its summer one that you might not think it was the same animal! This cat lives in pine forests across northern Europe and Asia. All year round, it has a short tail and tufts of fur on the tip of each ear. It can kill animals four times bigger than itself.

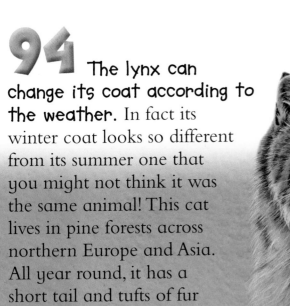

95 **One super–springy cat is the caracal.** It can leap an astonishing 3 metres into the air to swipe at a passing bird! A long time ago, this fine hunter was trained to catch birds and hares in India and Iran. Caracals live in dry, scrubby habitats which is why it has another name: the desert lynx.

◀ Wide, furry paws help prevent a lynx from sinking into the snow and give it a good grip on icy rocks.

A race against time

▲ When rainforests are cut down, millions of animals lose their homes.

96 Most of the big cats featured in this book are threatened with extinction. That means that they could disappear completely from the wild in the near future. One of the main reasons for this is the destruction of the big cats' habitat. All over the world, people and animals are fighting for space. Predators need plenty of space to hunt, but people need land to grow crops and graze cattle. Large areas of forest are also cut down to sell the trees or to search for valuable minerals underground.

I DON'T BELIEVE IT!
It is too late for some big cats. The Taiwan clouded leopard, the Caspian, Bali and Javan tigers are extinct. There are only about 260 Asiatic lions left in the wild.

97 It is the misfortune of many big cats that they have wonderful fur. For the last few hundred years, cats have been killed in their hundreds of thousands so that people can wear their skins. Most of this hunting is now against the law, but it still continues. Farmers also kill big cats that steal their cattle and other animals. These people need their animals to feed their families, or to sell to make money.

98

Wherever possible, zoos and wildlife parks keep big cats safe. Scientists help the animals to breed in the hope that one day they can be returned to the wild. It is not always so simple, though. Cheetahs and clouded leopards, for example, are very difficult to breed.

99

The Iberian lynx, which only lives in Spain and Portugal, is considered the most endangered of all the larger cats. It is now fully protected by law, but its habitat is so tiny that it doesn't have much chance of survival in the wild.

▲ The beautiful Iberian lynx mostly eats rabbits, deer and ducks. Cubs are usually born in April and stay with their mother until the following spring.

▼ Not long ago, people shot lions with guns. Now tourists come to Africa to shoot close-up photographs of big cats in their natural habitat.

100

The best way to shoot a big cat is through a camera lens. Tourists will pay a lot of money if they are promised the sight of a big cat. Now, in many places, the local people are doing everything they can to look after their wildlife so they can share it with visitors who come to their country.

Index